How to Draw Dolphins, Sharks, Whales and Other Sea Animals

First paperback edition May 2020

Book design by Aitz Marine

ISBN 9798644256389

This Grid Drawing Book

Belongs to

Let's Learn to Draw

Learning to draw is simple with the Grid Copy Method! The grid method has been used for hundreds of years by artists to simplify their work and is an excellent way to improve your observation and concentration, and a fun way to learn to draw simple objects.

Tips for Drawing

- Use light strokes. You can always go back and erase or darken your strokes!
- Sketch an outline first, then go back and detail.
- Don't forget to Count the squares carefully and to draw one square at a time.
- Practice, Practice, Practice makes Perfect!
- And take your time to master Drawing.

You will need 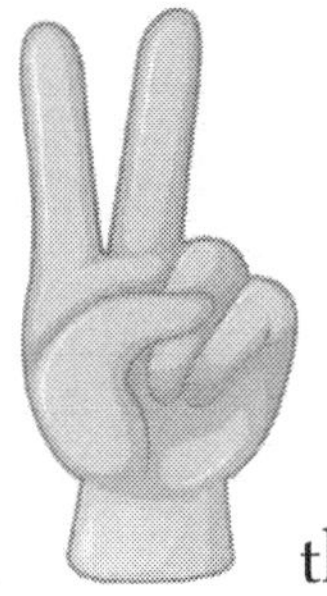 things: 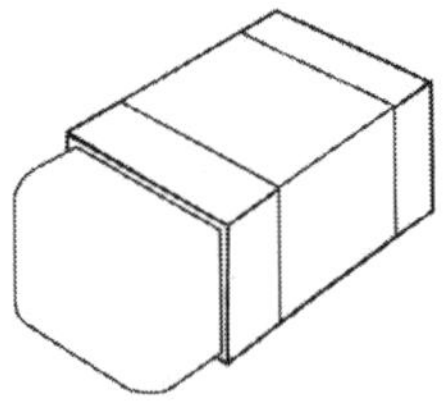 + 

Grab them, and Let's Start!

The Grid Drawing Method:

Grid drawing method is a technique that will help improve your accuracy without compromising the development of your freehand drawing in the long-term. It involves placing a grid over your image, then using that grid to assist with the placement of your drawing. It allows you to break the image down into smaller and more manageable segments or squares. Start with box A1 and work your way down to box M14, and try to sketch what you see in each box.

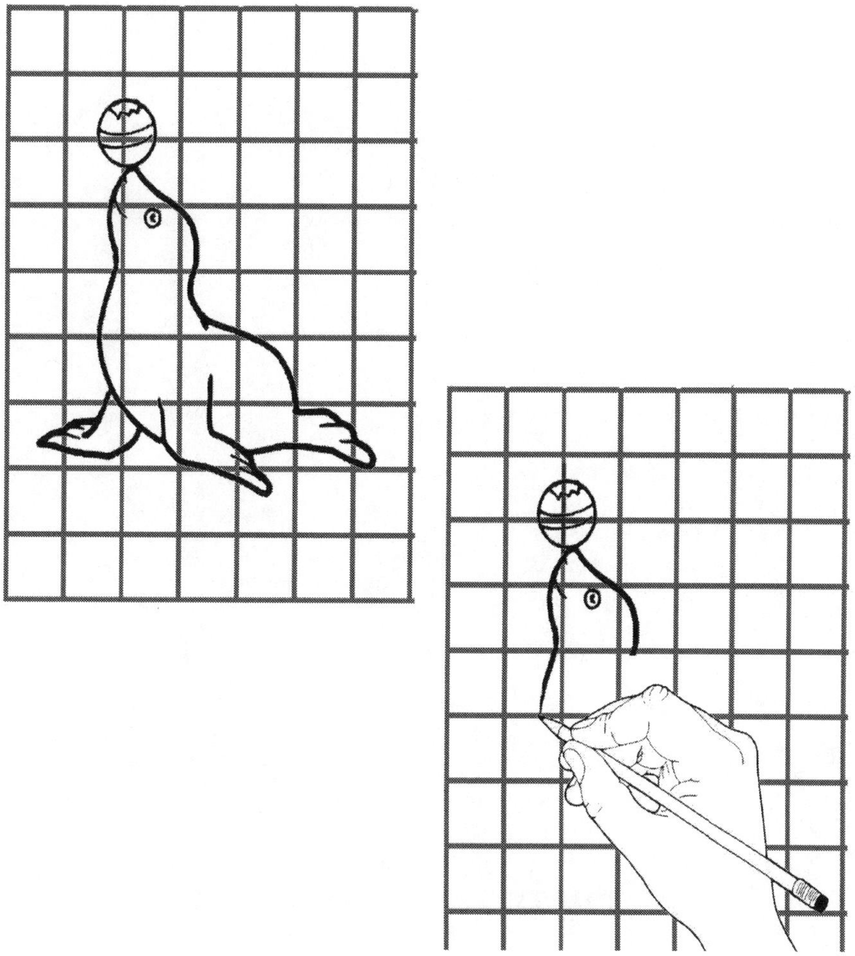

When you finish, COLOR YOUR ART.

SEA SHELL

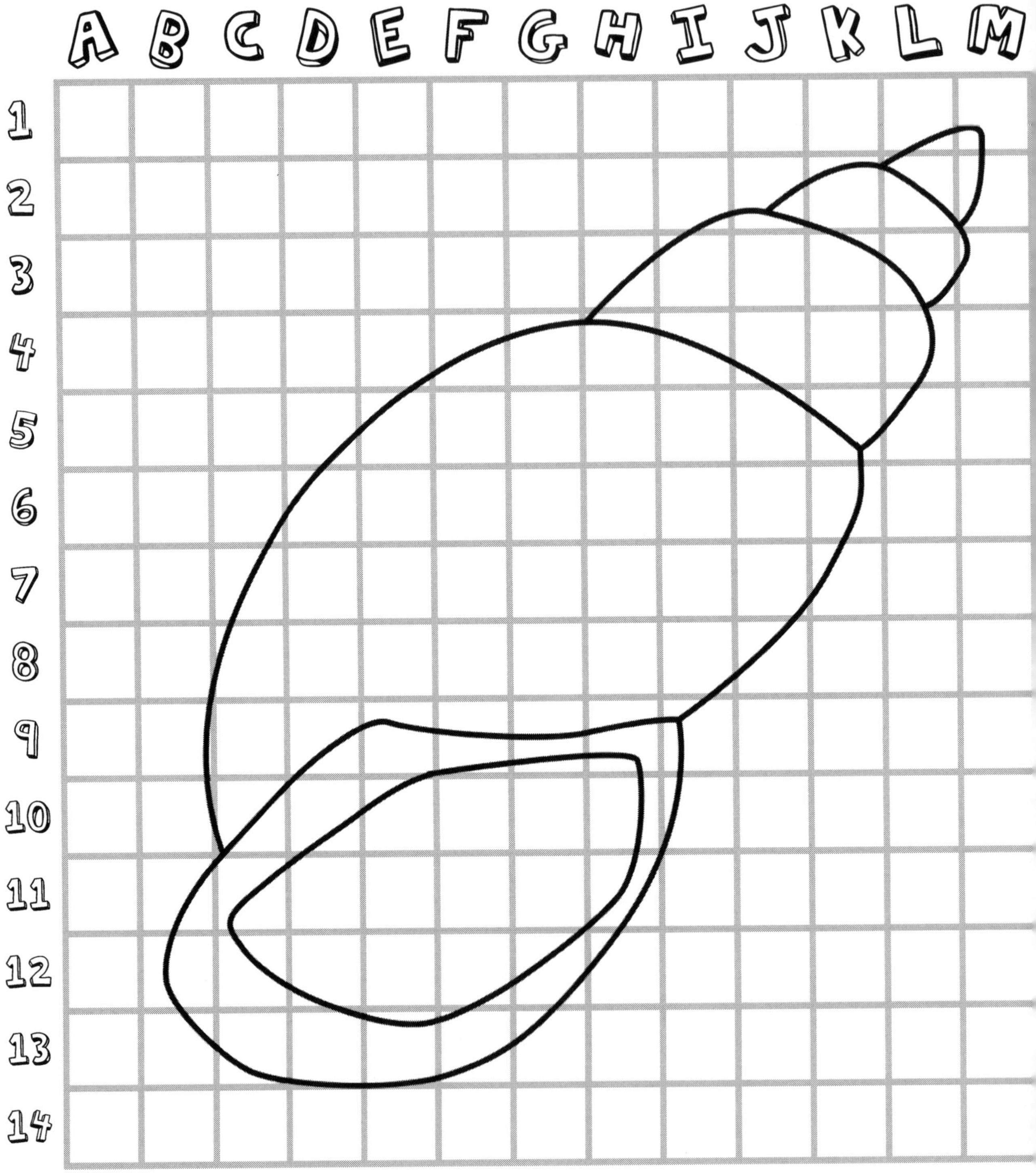

	A	B	C	D	E	F	G	H	I	J	K	L	M
1													
2													
3													
4													
5													
6													
7													
8													
9													
10													
11													
12													
13													
14													

SEA SHELL

	A	B	C	D	E	F	G	H	I	J	K	L	M
1													
2													
3													
4													
5													
6													
7													
8													
9													
10													
11													
12													
13													
14													

SHARK

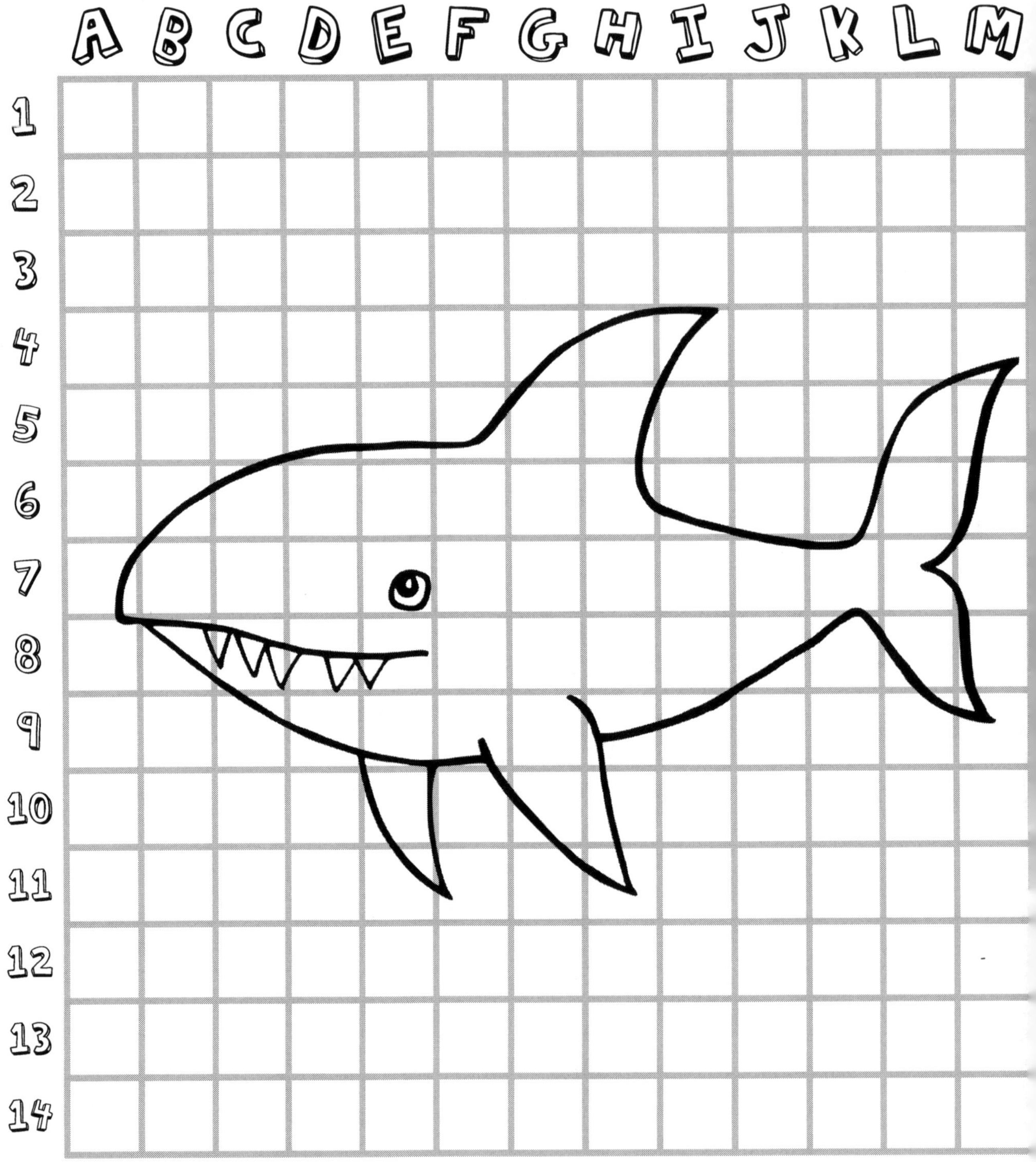

	A	B	C	D	E	F	G	H	I	J	K	L	M
1													
2													
3													
4													
5													
6													
7													
8													
9													
10													
11													
12													
13													
14													

SEASTAR

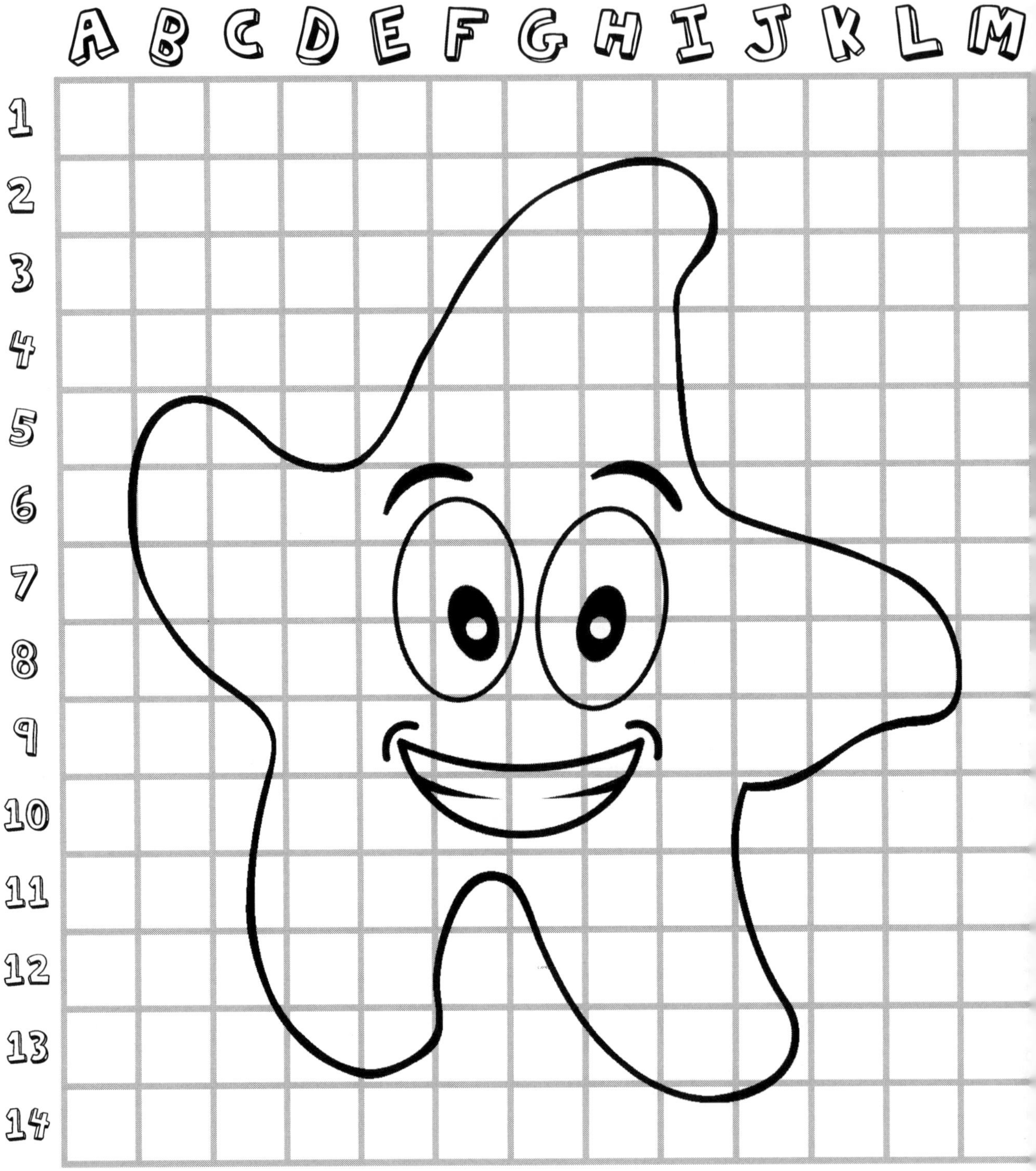

	A	B	C	D	E	F	G	H	I	J	K	L	M
1													
2													
3													
4													
5													
6													
7													
8													
9													
10													
11													
12													
13													
14													

SEA TURTLE

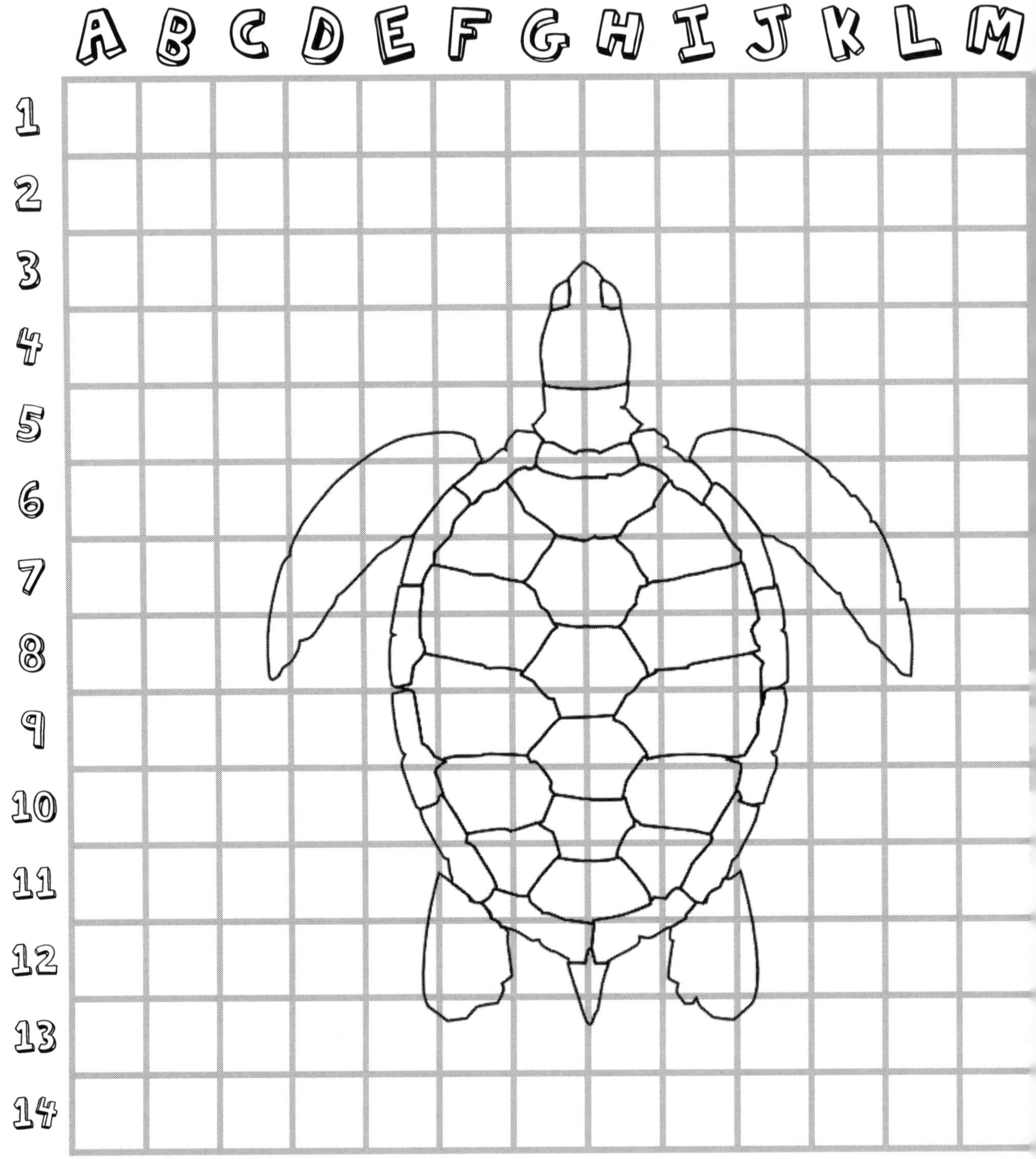

	A	B	C	D	E	F	G	H	I	J	K	L	M
1													
2													
3													
4													
5													
6													
7													
8													
9													
10													
11													
12													
13													
14													

PENGUIN

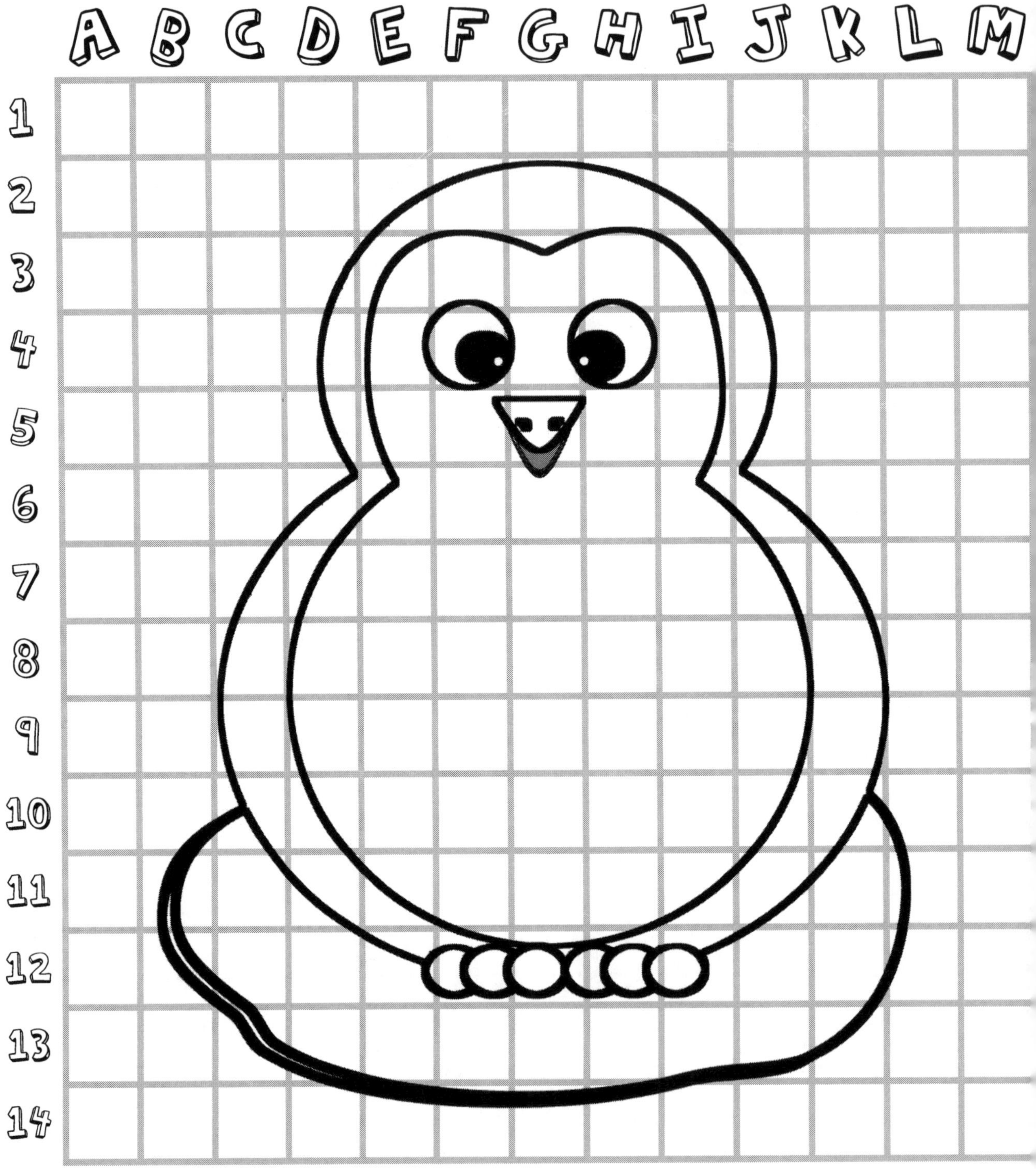

	A	B	C	D	E	F	G	H	I	J	K	L	M
1													
2													
3													
4													
5													
6													
7													
8													
9													
10													
11													
12													
13													
14													

WHALE

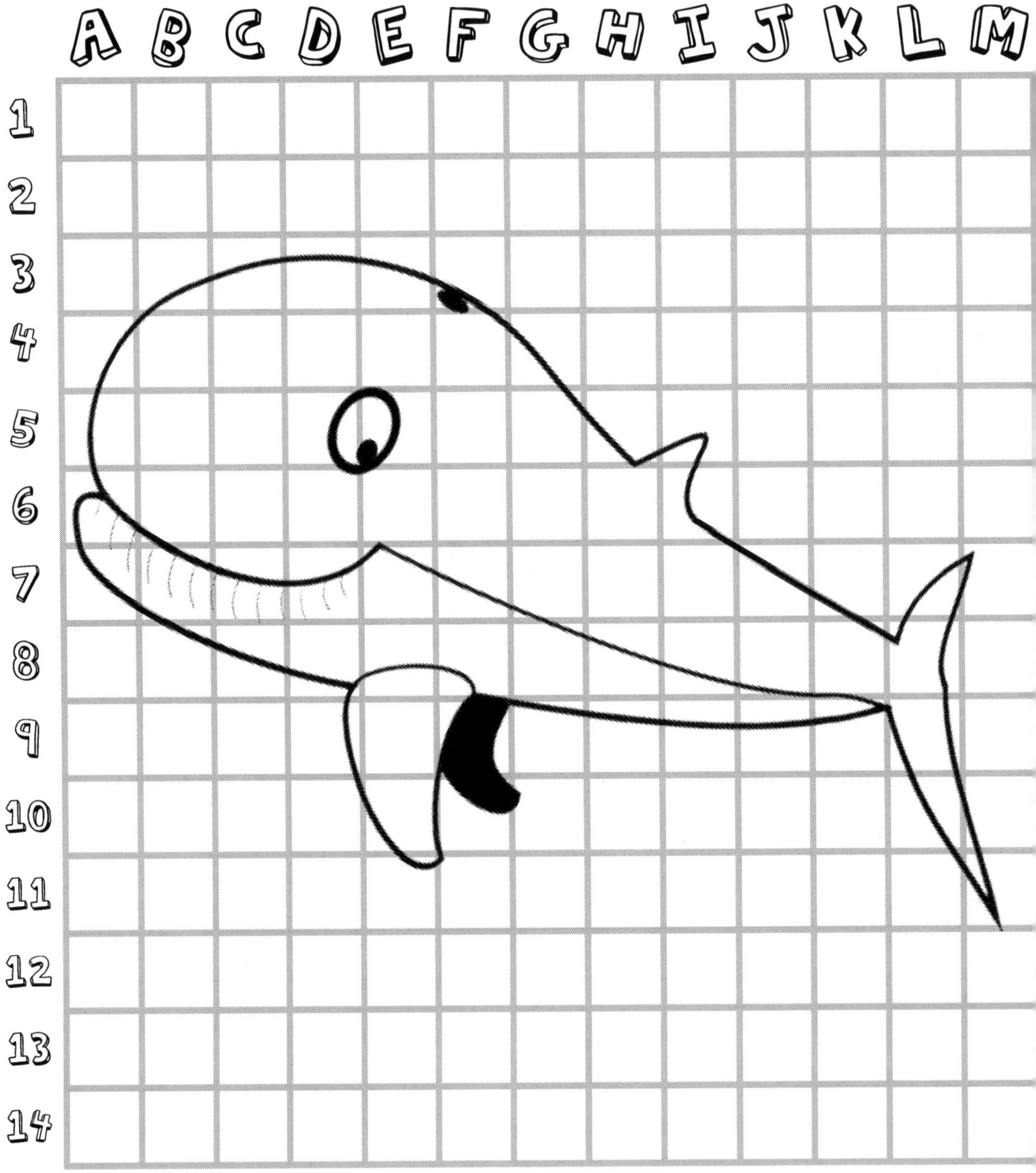

	A	B	C	D	E	F	G	H	I	J	K	L	M
1													
2													
3													
4													
5													
6													
7													
8													
9													
10													
11													
12													
13													
14													

FISH

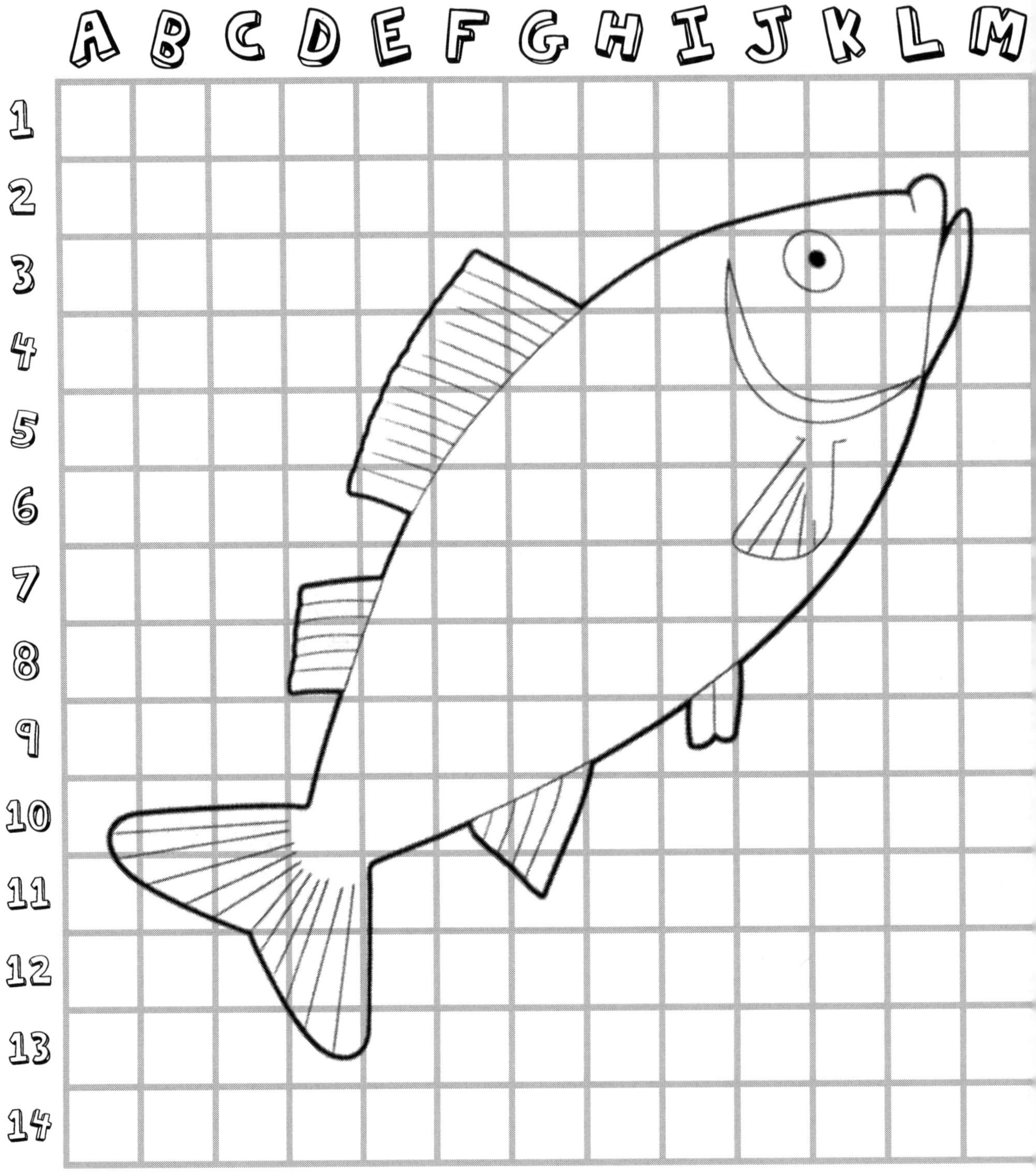

	A	B	C	D	E	F	G	H	I	J	K	L	M
1													
2													
3													
4													
5													
6													
7													
8													
9													
10													
11													
12													
13													
14													

FISH

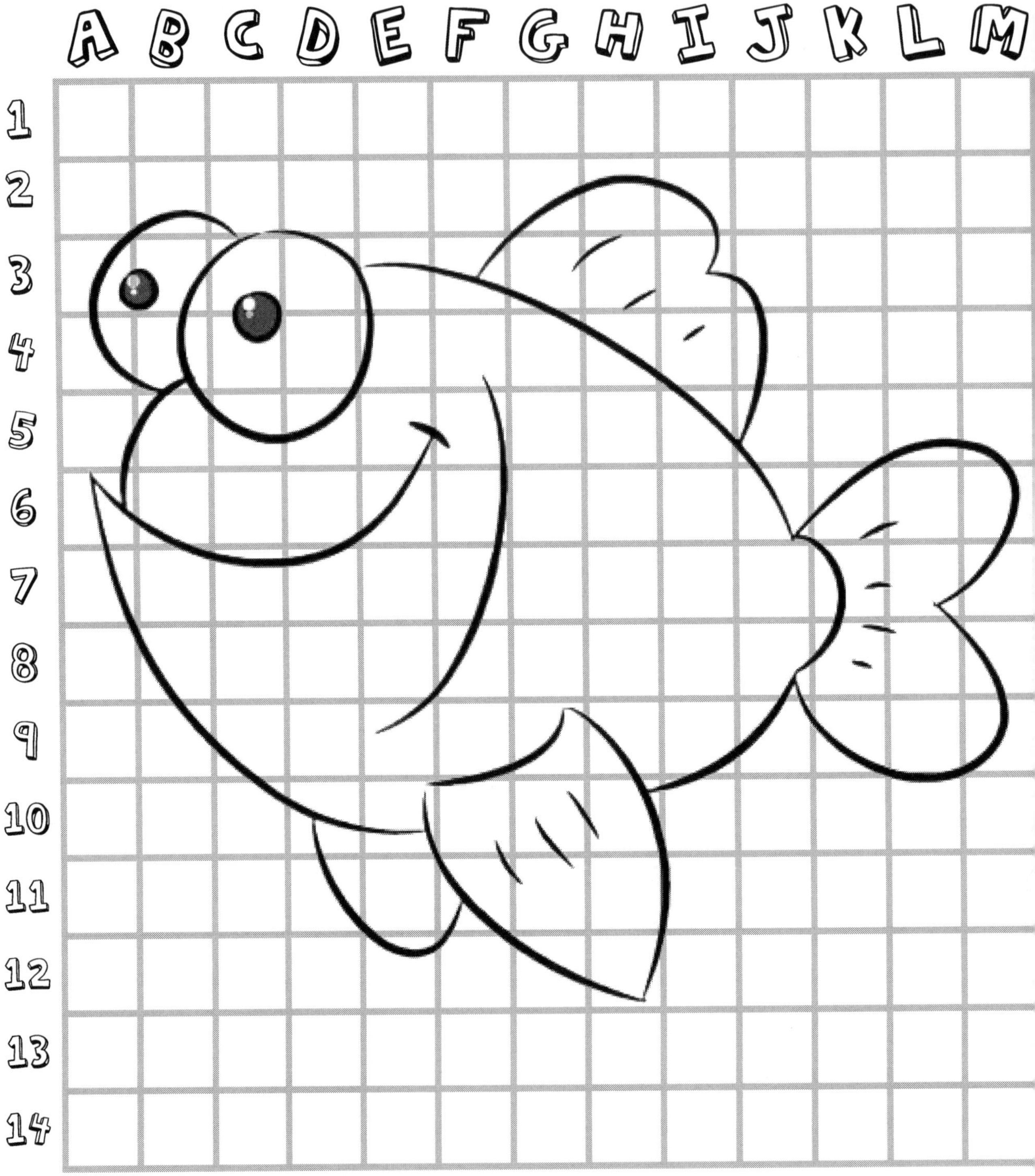

	A	B	C	D	E	F	G	H	I	J	K	L	M
1													
2													
3													
4													
5													
6													
7													
8													
9													
10													
11													
12													
13													
14													

OCTOPUS

	A	B	C	D	E	F	G	H	I	J	K	L	M
1													
2													
3													
4													
5													
6													
7													
8													
9													
10													
11													
12													
13													
14													

FISH

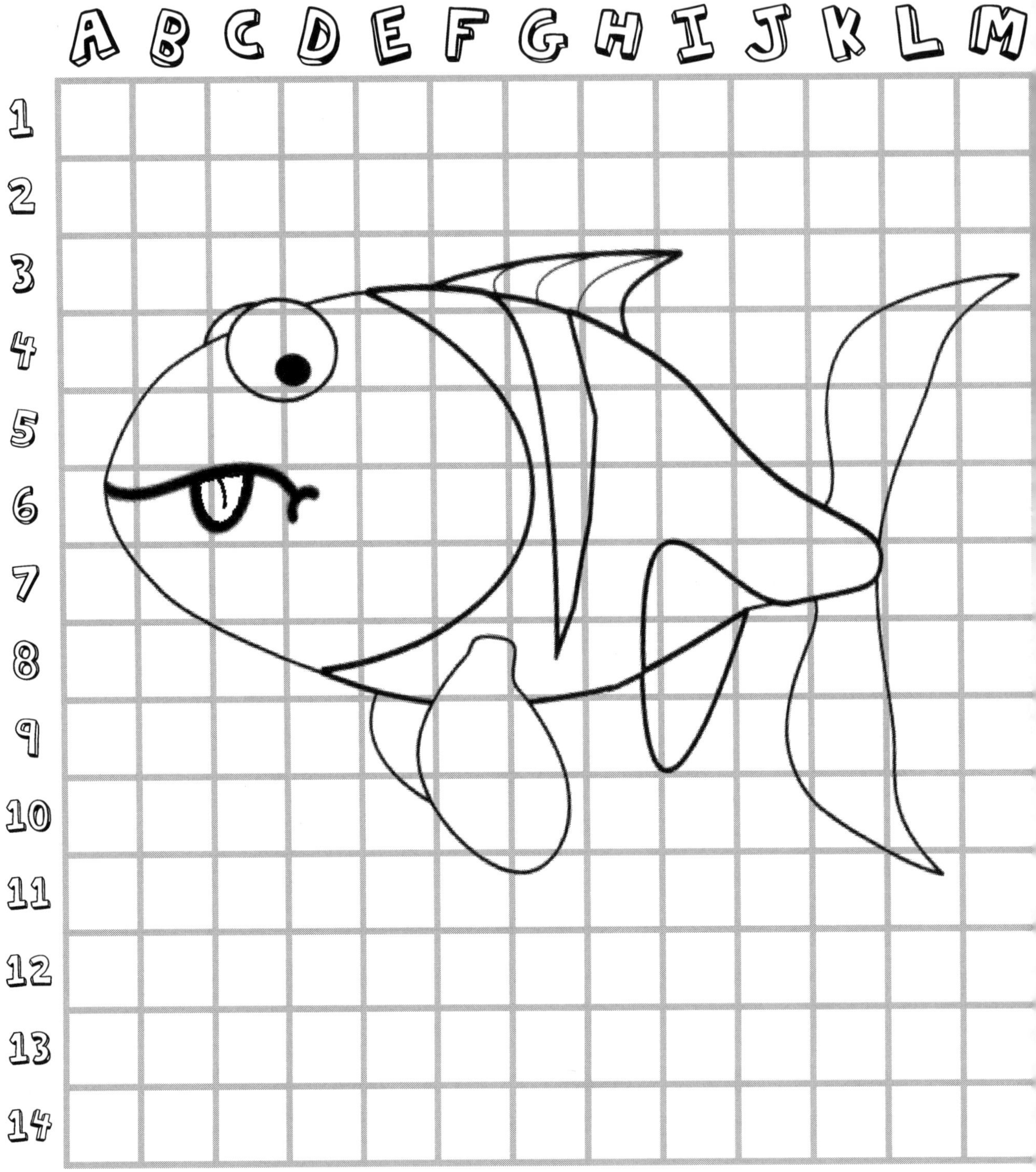

	A	B	C	D	E	F	G	H	I	J	K	L	M
1													
2													
3													
4													
5													
6													
7													
8													
9													
10													
11													
12													
13													
14													

PIRANHA

	A	B	C	D	E	F	G	H	I	J	K	L	M
1													
2													
3													
4													
5													
6													
7													
8													
9													
10													
11													
12													
13													
14													

WALRUS

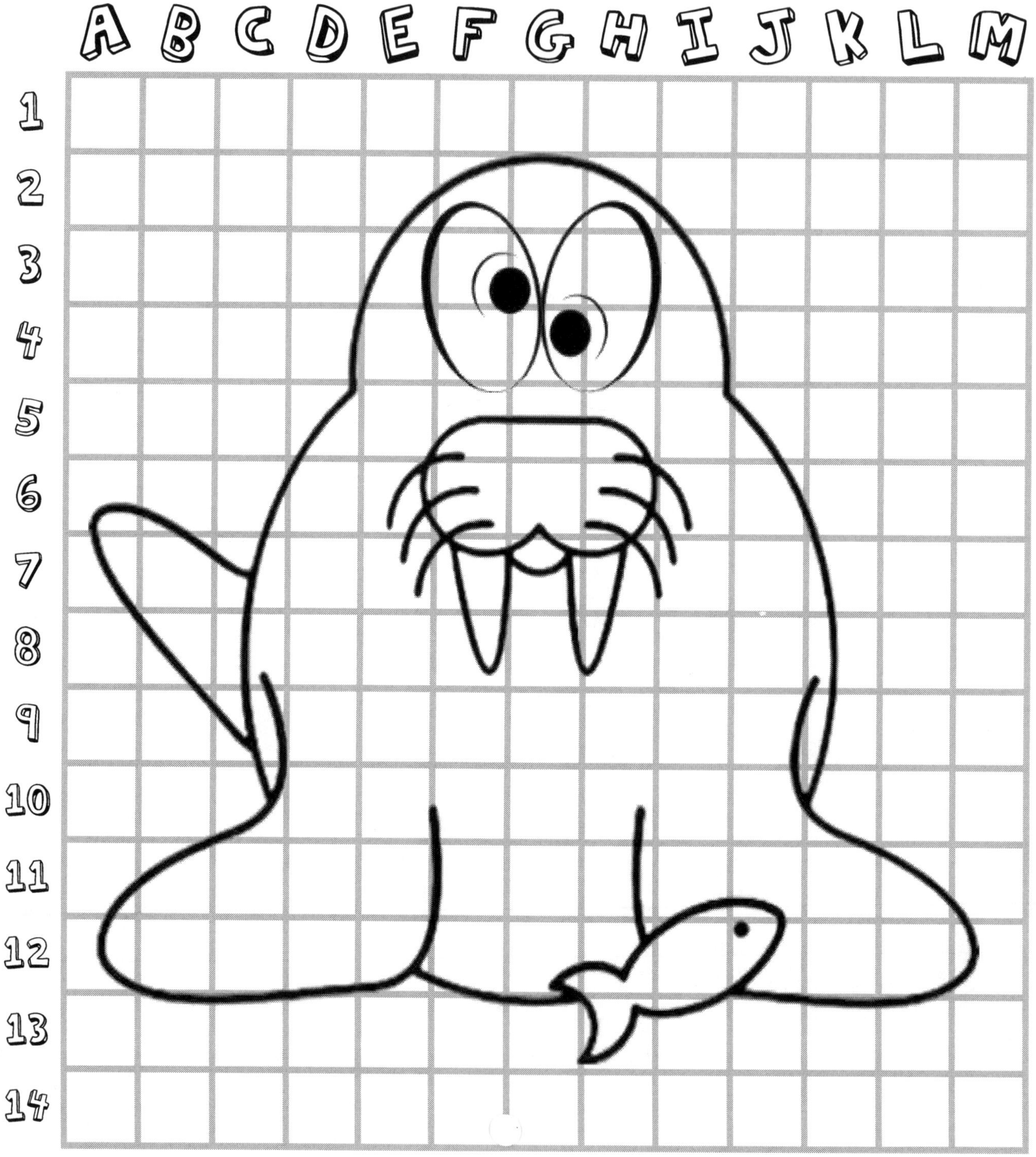

	A	B	C	D	E	F	G	H	I	J	K	L	M
1													
2													
3													
4													
5													
6													
7													
8													
9													
10													
11													
12													
13													
14													

FISH

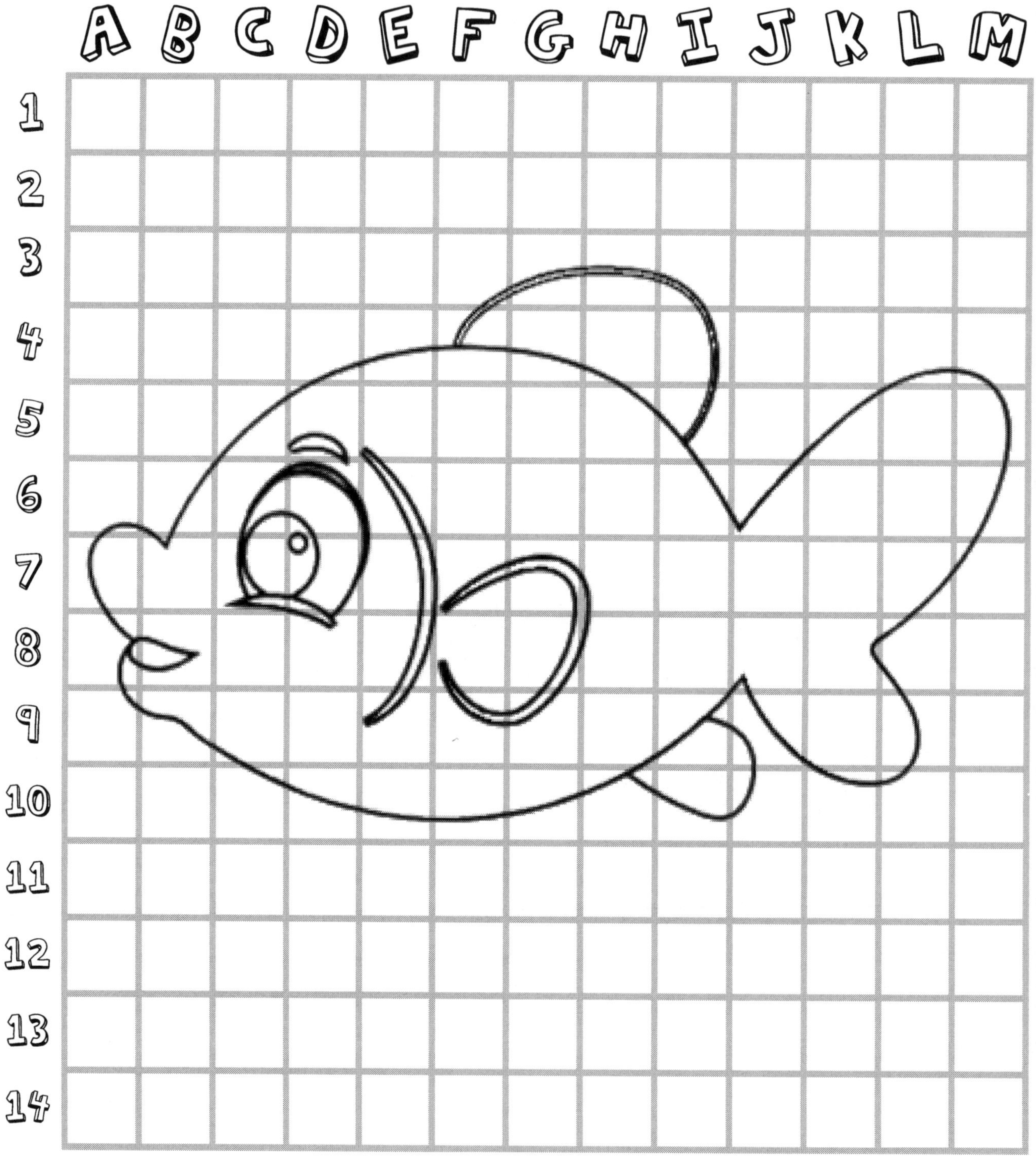

	A	B	C	D	E	F	G	H	I	J	K	L	M
1													
2													
3													
4													
5													
6													
7													
8													
9													
10													
11													
12													
13													
14													

FISH

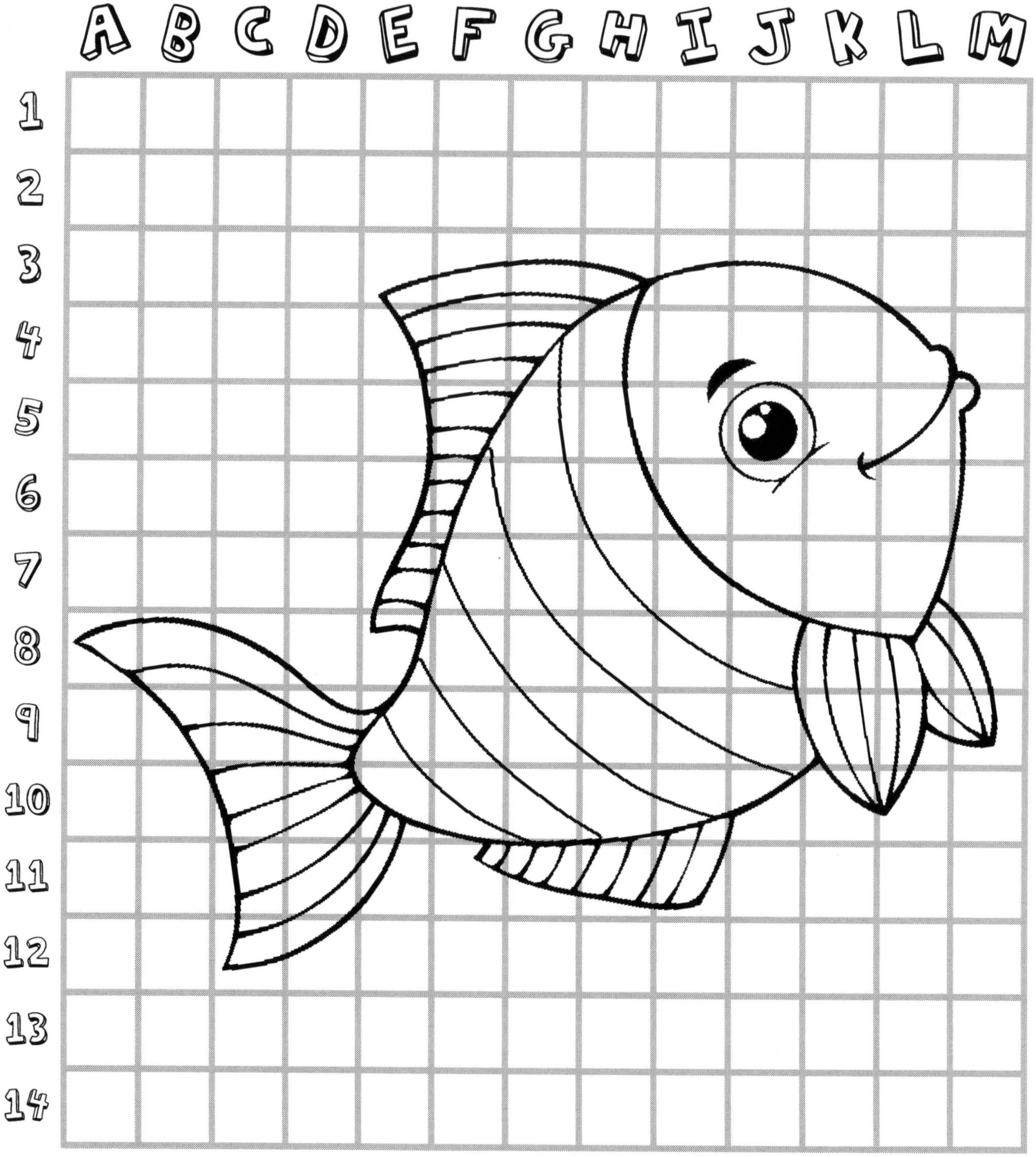

	A	B	C	D	E	F	G	H	I	J	K	L	M
1													
2													
3													
4													
5													
6													
7													
8													
9													
10													
11													
12													
13													
14													

SQUID

	A	B	C	D	E	F	G	H	I	J	K	L	M
1													
2													
3													
4													
5													
6													
7													
8													
9													
10													
11													
12													
13													
14													

FISH

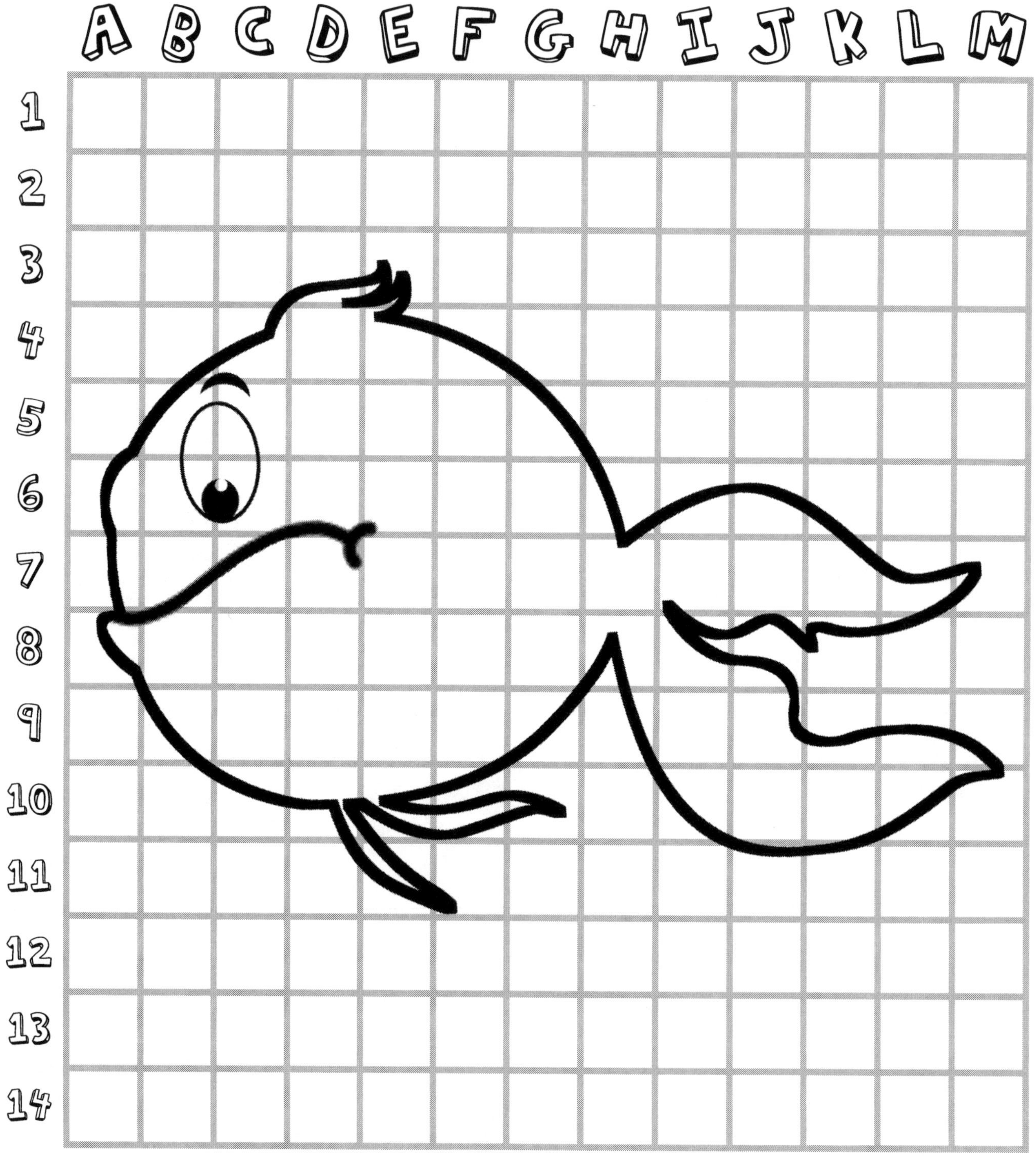

	A	B	C	D	E	F	G	H	I	J	K	L	M
1													
2													
3													
4													
5													
6													
7													
8													
9													
10													
11													
12													
13													
14													

SEAL

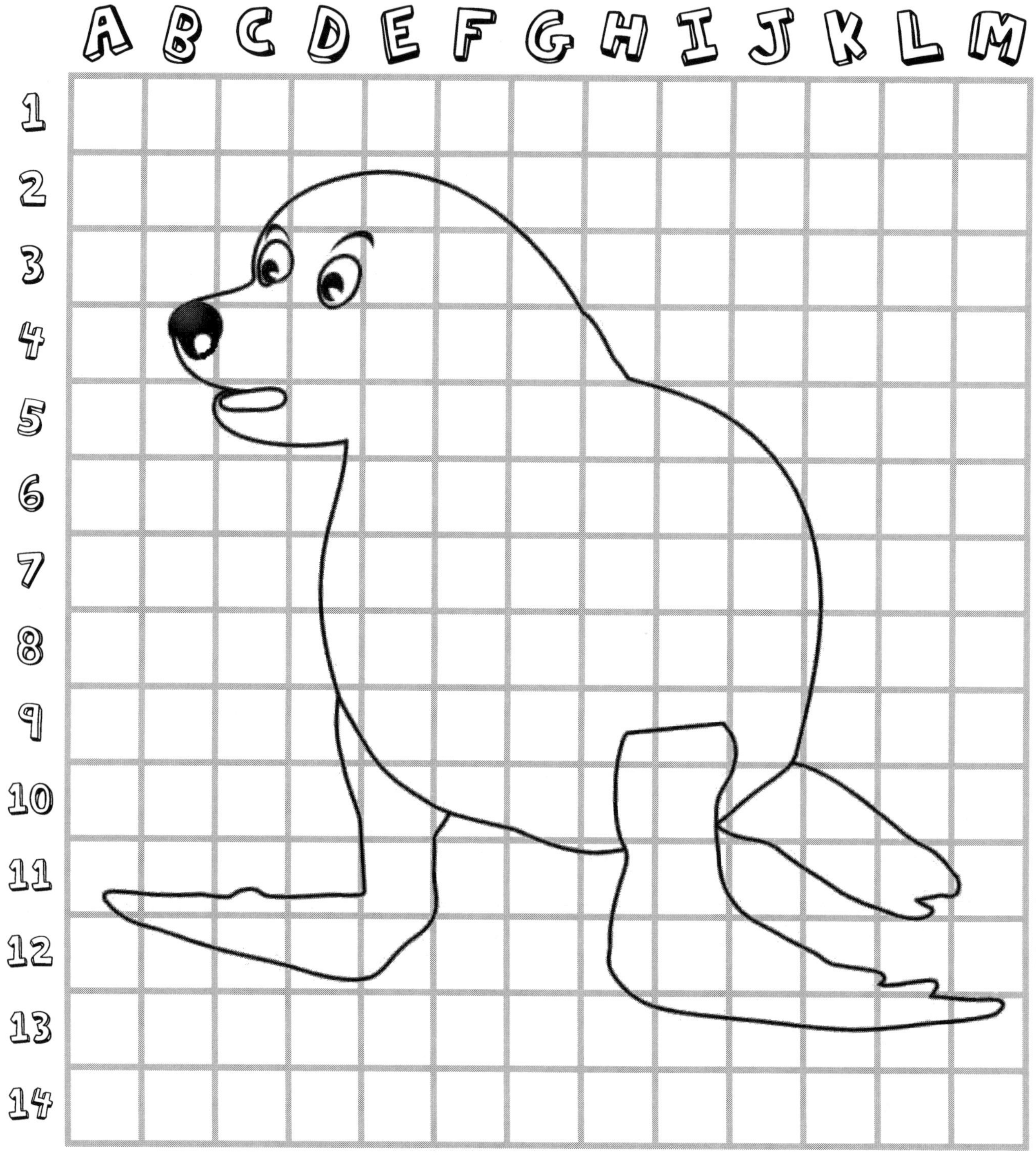

	A	B	C	D	E	F	G	H	I	J	K	L	M
1													
2													
3													
4													
5													
6													
7													
8													
9													
10													
11													
12													
13													
14													

SEA TURTLE

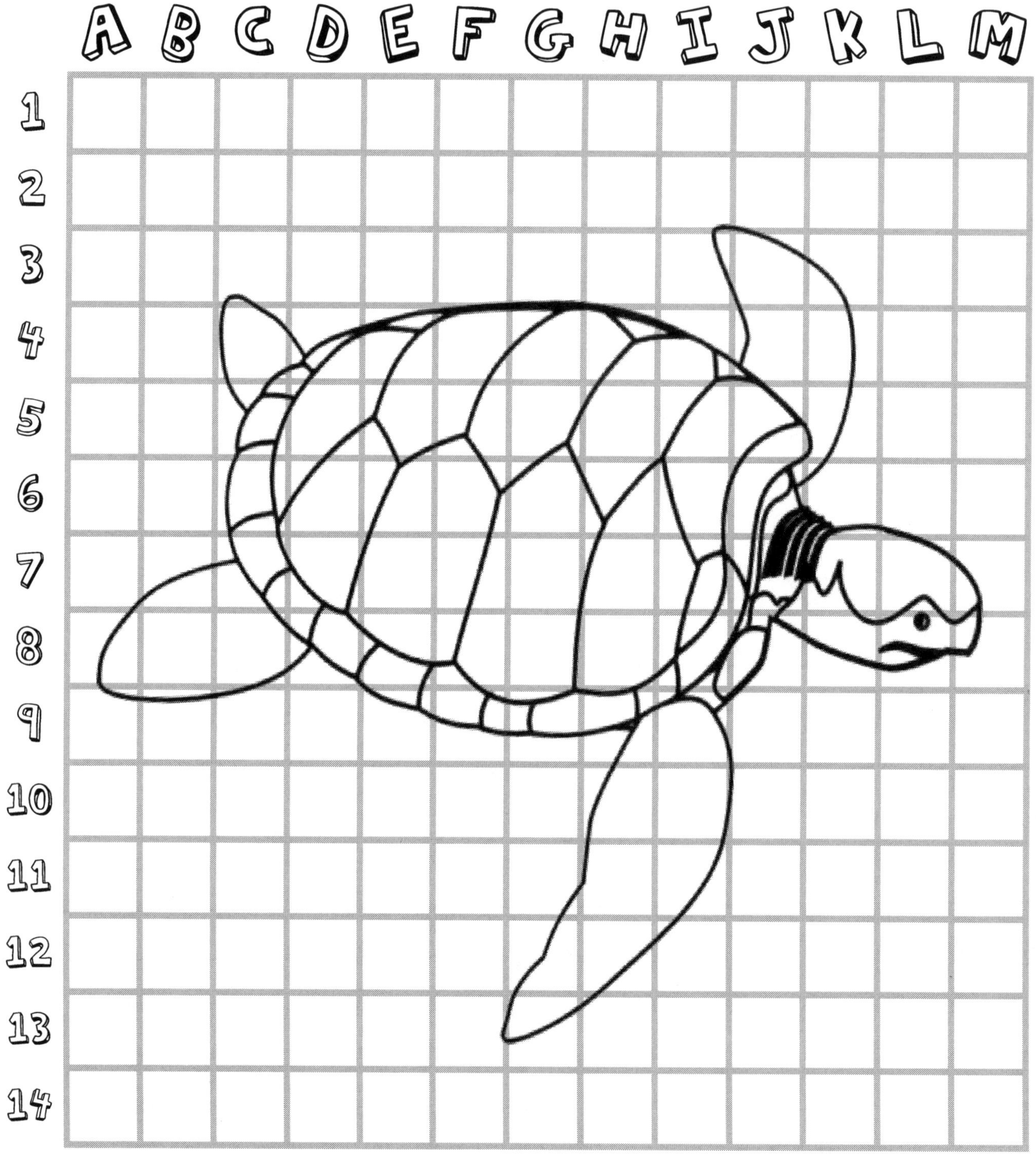

	A	B	C	D	E	F	G	H	I	J	K	L	M
1													
2													
3													
4													
5													
6													
7													
8													
9													
10													
11													
12													
13													
14													

PENGUIN

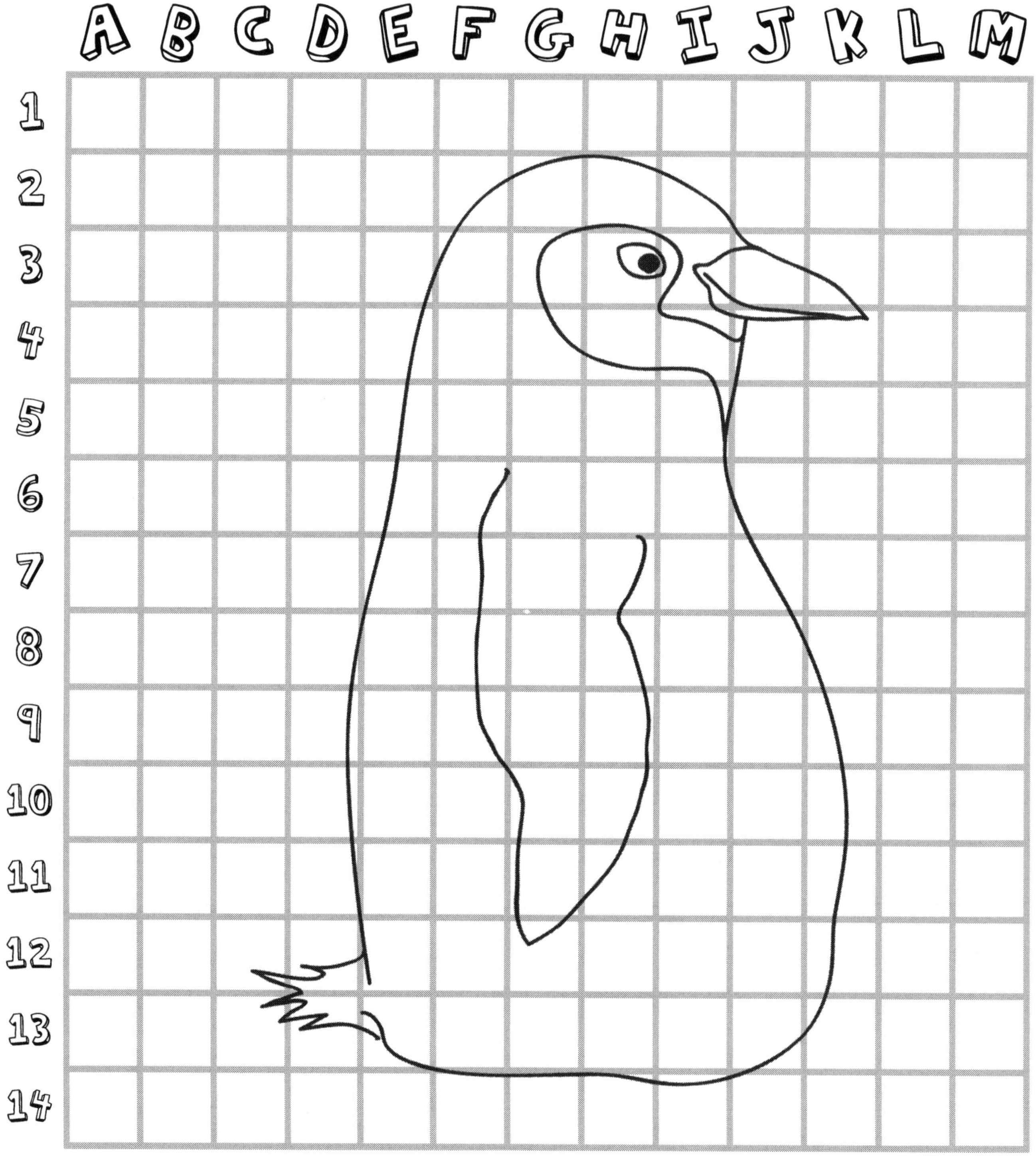

	A	B	C	D	E	F	G	H	I	J	K	L	M
1													
2													
3													
4													
5													
6													
7													
8													
9													
10													
11													
12													
13													
14													

ISLAND

	A	B	C	D	E	F	G	H	I	J	K	L	M
1													
2													
3													
4													
5													
6													
7													
8													
9													
10													
11													
12													
13													
14													

FISH

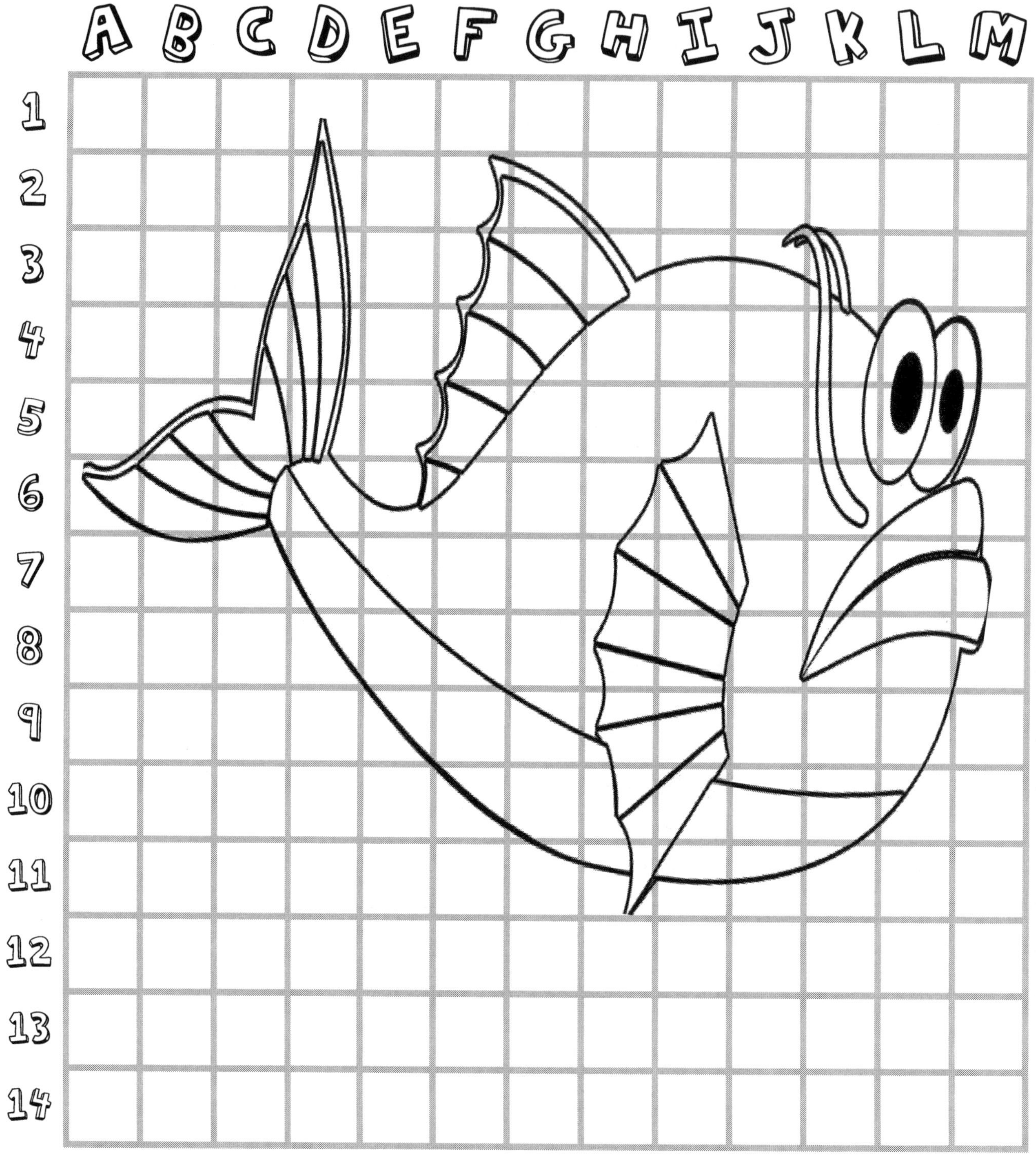

	A	B	C	D	E	F	G	H	I	J	K	L	M
1													
2													
3													
4													
5													
6													
7													
8													
9													
10													
11													
12													
13													
14													

DOLPHIN

	A	B	C	D	E	F	G	H	I	J	K	L	M
1													
2													
3													
4													
5													
6													
7													
8													
9													
10													
11													
12													
13													
14													

FISH

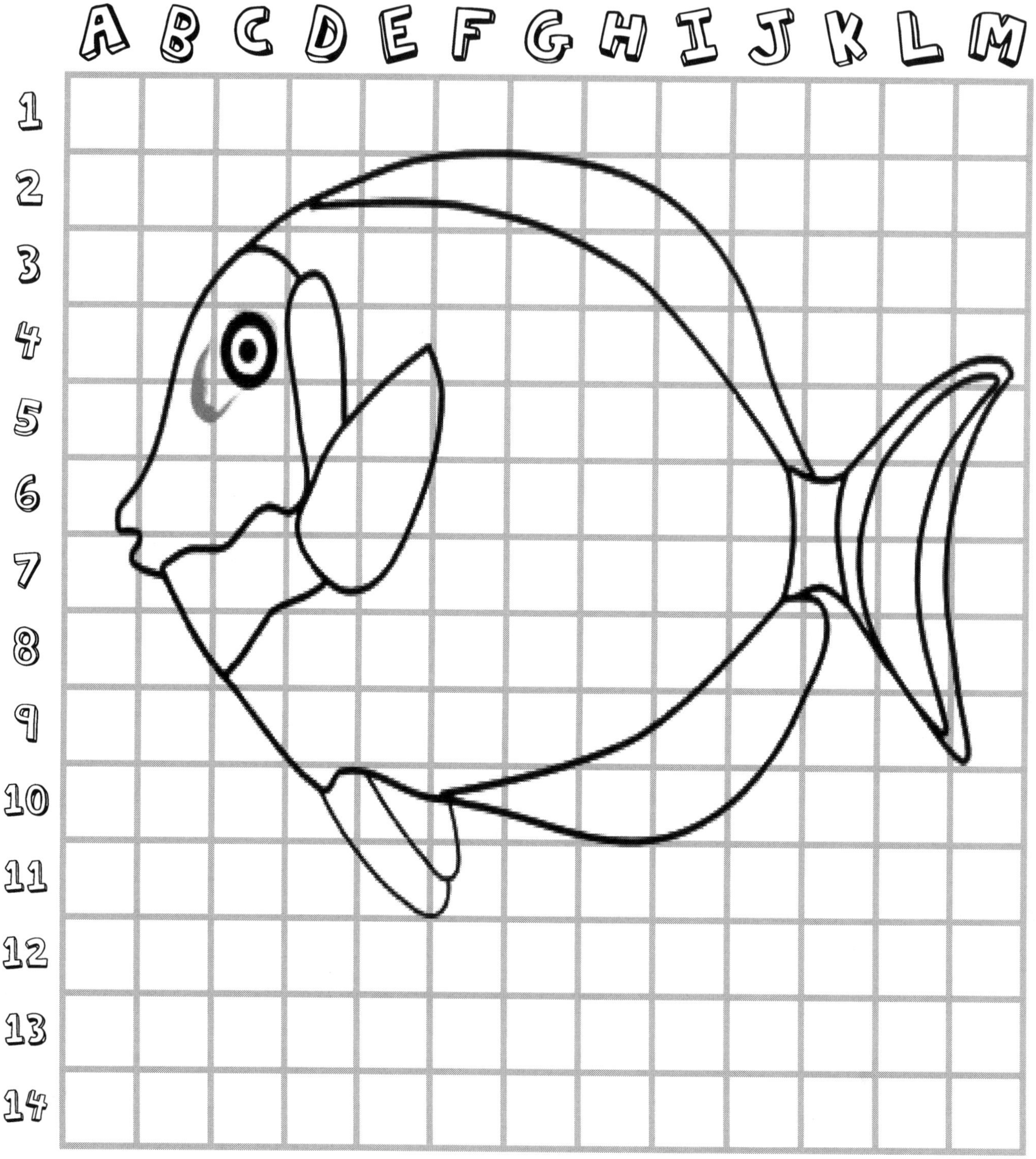

	A	B	C	D	E	F	G	H	I	J	K	L	M
1													
2													
3													
4													
5													
6													
7													
8													
9													
10													
11													
12													
13													
14													

SEAHORSE

	A	B	C	D	E	F	G	H	I	J	K	L	M
1													
2													
3													
4													
5													
6													
7													
8													
9													
10													
11													
12													
13													
14													

Made in the USA
Columbia, SC
09 December 2024

48912670R00030